THE UNBREAKABLE WOMAN SERIES

BEGIN WITH BELIEF

TINA FOBBS

Tina Fobbs
Presents

The Unbreakable Woman Series
Book One: Begin with Belief

Written By
Tina M. Fobbs

❀ Created with Vellum

PRELUDE

The purpose of The Unbreakable Woman Book Series is to remind the everyday, strong woman that she can, and she will have more because no matter what she goes through, she is unbreakable. Only you and God can determine what your life is destined to be. Never forget that.

You are a beautiful woman and sometimes you just have to say "yes" to yourself.

Yes, I can do it.
Yes, I can be it.
Yes, I deserve it.
Yes, I can have it.

Be proud of yourself for even trying to make the shift in mindset to always believe in yourself. No, it doesn't happen overnight. Self-doubt has taken over the best of us, but you must begin with belief, trust the process, and understand that you, myself, and all the women who hold us up can make the impossible, possible. The first installment of *The Unbreakable Woman Book Series* is entitled *Begin with Belief*, because it shows how we refuse to let unthinkable situations stop us from being the best version of ourselves.

I am writing this book to you to serve as the beginning of the re-awakening of your endless possibilities, lead you to making bold decisions, recommit to yourself, and use your power unapologetically.

Do you know that you have power? Power means the ability to make things happen or the ability to cause change. My unbreakable woman, why are you sitting on your power? This book will help you activate your power and create a positive change in your life and those around you. There's always more to life than what you have now. You are just scratching the surface.

1

"The best way to predict the future is to create it."

When you can sit down, breathe, relax, and just feel free. How does that life feel to you? When it comes to financial freedom, many people think that securing a position at the high paying job is exactly what they need to feel that liberty. There would be no worries about bills, kids would be happy, there is extra money to take trips with friends etc.

I've always been somewhat rebellious. I've always hated working an actual nine to five. When I did, it was to feel what others called *normal*. As I got older I was certain that I needed a new normal. Where I was from, saying you were an entrepreneur was another way of saying you were in between jobs. Not for me. I could easily find jobs. I was young and educated.

It seemed like it was such a big deal to have a college degree. If you are reading this, and you've graduated from college, you know what I'm talking about. That day you walk across the stage you feel like you're on top of the world. Even the day after when you wake up and you just feel like a brand new, accomplished person. Then when someone asks, "How are you?" your answer is "I'm great. I just graduated from college." They say congratulations, but they really want to say, "Who cares?" It's probably because they know, just like after you consume that 5-Hour Energy drink and it starts to wear off, your graduation high is coming down slowly but surely. It happened to me just like that!

I was ecstatic when I graduated, and I was getting ready to be a new mom. I interned at a major radio station the year before which turned into me having a show with a few other ladies. I got a bachelor's degree in Mass Communication with a concentration in radio production, so it seemed as if I had everything figured out. That's until I realized I really didn't care for radio. It just wasn't for me. I wasn't one who really enjoyed being in the limelight. I didn't want to do the kind of work it required to be successful in that industry. I didn't even like hearing the sound of my voice playing back on the radio in the commercials that I had done. It was awful. Although I made some awesome connections, some of whom I'm still very close to now, I'm glad I walked away from it. But where did that leave me? LOST.

Aside from being an assistant at a hair salon, radio was all I had ever done. People go to school for four plus years and have no clue what to do when they graduate. That's how so many of us end up in debt and stuck having a degree that is doing nothing for us. Had I known, I would have had a mentor to show me the way.

"Every successful person was once an unknown person who refused to give up on their dreams."

LATER, I found out that this is the part where jobs take over your life and you start trading your time for money. I hated it. I was a new mom and working all day. My parents, may God rest their souls, were slaves to societal norms. My mother was a high school graduate and my father had a middle school education. So, the thought of their children graduating from college and landing it *"big"* was amazing to them. I was the last of their five children, the only girl, and the first to graduate college. The pressure was on! Having a job with benefits was exactly where I should have been. It was great until I was introduced to a different lifestyle. Entrepreneurship.

I knew early on that entrepreneurship was my way out.

Figuring out what I was going to do was the hard part. One of the greatest feelings in the world is experiencing that paradigm shift from employee to entrepreneur. Making the change from the steady life of a full-time employee to the unpredictable world of entrepreneurship requires a shift of mind that many people tend to overlook. Not only do you have to change your mindset, but you have to know exactly what your best life, your life of freedom, looks like to you. That's the part they left out. The vision.

"The richest people in the world build networks, others look for work."

I BEGAN my new journey when I was about twenty-five years old. Anyone who knows me understands that I'm far from the girly girl type. I could care less about name brand clothes, purses or shoes. So, that makes me ask this one question. Why did I open a shoe store?

It really wasn't me. I figured that since I was bored and already had money, it seemed like a great idea. More importantly, it felt safe to me. Looking back on things now, I count that as a fun adventure. Why? Because I had no marketing plan. Never even thought about marketing. The large, loyal customer base I did have was all by luck.

I had mastered the art of finding my target audience and speaking directly to them. It was perfect. I would partner with promoters, managers, and event planners every week. They would give twenty percent off cards for my store at their establishments to their clients or have that as a door prize. My logo would be on their flyers and websites. It was genius. No promotion costs on my end. But that wasn't fulfilling. It just wasn't me. I had to be clearer on what I wanted and that's exactly what I want you to do now.

Take the time to really think about all the things you want out of life. Whether it's what you want in the next two weeks, the next two months or the next two years, it's important for you to take the steps necessary to have all that you desire. Never be afraid to ask for exactly what you want. Right now I want you to think about what would make you happy and write it down.

2

"What you think is what you are."

I am a big dreamer and I know this world is plentiful. There is so much out here for you, so what are you giving yourself permission to have? What conversation are you having with yourself?

If you ever tell yourself you can't accomplish something, it's important that you change the conversation. To speak is to create. Your words are even more powerful than your thoughts. You must mentally be a winner before you can actually win. If your checkbook is negative, your car is broken down, your husband is leaving, whatever the situation, you have to remain in the mindset of a winner.

My thing was, I refused to be average. I wanted to **rise** in every meaning of the word. One: to move from a lower position to a higher one. I no longer wanted to feel stuck in place. I wanted to move beyond what was expected of me. Two: get up from lying, sitting or kneeling. I needed to move. I couldn't lie down and wait for things to change. I couldn't continue to pray for God to send me the winning lottery ticket. If I was going to pray I had to take action as well. Finally, three: an increase in amount. In the eyes of some people I was financially comfortable, but for myself, I needed an increase.

No one wants to be the average person living the average life. They may tell you that but no one wants that. That's just what they settle for. That's what people have put as the cap on their happiness. Not me. I dream every day. I'm always wanting to do something new and I know I can do it. If I can't do it yet, I'm always certain that I know someone who is willing to teach me. So why in the world would I set limitations for myself? I'm thinking big and I encourage you to do the same. Surround yourself with positivity as you are dreaming your wildest dreams.

Any time you think of something that changes your attitude or changes the way you are feeling in that moment, it is a thought that clearly affects you. If this is a negative effect, you must do whatever it is you have to do to try to remove that thought. Create thoughts that bring the most joy to your life.

Don't think about how broke you are, how much you don't have, how small your house is, how old your car is.

Whatever you think about, you bring about. I know it's easier said than done to find that happy place but think about this: you are still living and breathing. *You have life*! There is nothing more joyous than knowing that you have been given another day to be great, to be fearless, and to *begin with belief*.

3

"Faith is to believe what you do not see; the reward is to see what you believe."

Have you ever heard someone use the term "fake it 'til you make it?" While I don't necessarily agree with the thought of faking it, I do believe that this term goes hand in hand with visualization. This is the best way to think about yourself in a positive light. Visualizing is the key to mentally seeing and orienting our lives toward our goals. The longer you hold a mental picture in your mind the harder it is for your brain to differentiate what is imagined and what is real.

Imagine yourself overcoming that feeling of inferiority.

You may be in a bad place emotionally but there is never a wrong time to #BeginWithBelief. Visualize yourself in a different place. A place that is exactly where you want to be in life rather than where you are right now. This is called the theory of self-actualization which was created by Abraham Maslow. He describes the good life as one directed towards self-actualization, the pinnacle need. Self-actualization occurs when you maximize your potential by doing the best that you can do. I'm going to share with you some character-istics of a self-actualized person (paraphrased of course). Does this sound like you?

▶ THESE PEOPLE have a realistic perception of their own selves, of others, as well as the world around them.

▶ THEY ARE able to accept people as well as their own selves along with their flaws. The shortcomings and other flawed factors are accepted with tolerance and humor.

▶ THEY HAVE great problem-solving skills, which means that not only are they able to solve their own problems, they are also able to (and want to) help others in the world.

.   .   .

► THEY RELY on their own judgment and intelligence to form opinions about people and things. They are not influenced by the external environment, or the people in it.

► THEY ARE EXTREMELY spontaneous in their attitude and never succumb to the pressures of how others want them to behave. However, they are also known to abide by the law.

► WHILE THEY can do extremely well in group settings, they require time to be by themselves so that they can work on developing their own individual potential.

► THESE PEOPLE have an innocent look towards life, where they are able to appreciate something with the same intensity every time they look at it.

► NOT ONLY ARE THEY able to find and appreciate the humor in the world and in other people, they are also able to laugh at themselves.

► SELF-ACTUALIZERS FORM DEEP, meaningful interpersonal relationships in life.

. . .

▶ THEY ARE KNOWN to have peak experiences which are occasions marked by feelings of harmony, deep meaning, and ecstasy. These experiences leave them feeling one with the universe, calmer, full of positivity, love, purpose, and a profusion of several other positive emotions.

"A lack of clarity can put the brakes on any journey to success."

I'M NOT GOING to get all scientific on you. I just wanted you to know a little bit about self-actualization. That is something you can look up and read about later. Continue to paint your vision in your mind. This involves you getting clear on what you want. You have to know where it is you want to be in order to get there.

This is especially true if you want to start a business or even get a major promotion at work. There are many people who don't know exactly what they want, they just know that they want something else. This usually leaves them feeling stuck.

Being stuck is a sign that you have abandoned what matters most to you and what you wanted to accomplish in life. If you continue to ignore yourself and what you love to do, your entire life will suffer in different areas. You won't always realize that your disappointment in yourself is what is causing disappointment all around you. So, let's cut that out now and start putting yourself first.

"When life gets blurry, adjust your focus."

BE SELFISH IN YOUR CLARITY. Design something that fits you. If you're thinking about diving into entrepreneurship, build something that supports your needs and takes into consideration your gifts and talents. Who wants to begin creating a failing empire? No one.

When you first start out you will receive all kinds of advice from everyone. Insights will come from less than qualified, but equally opinionated influential people who urge you to start doing things their way. You will have to decide which pieces of advice to apply and which ones to release. Don't be the person who takes advice from everyone and end up with a business that you're not comfortable talking about because you can't quite explain what you do. Building something you love involves finding your inner passion.

"Faith plus laziness equals stress."

SOMETIMES FINDING your passion and purpose can seem difficult. We all have unique gifts that we were put on this earth to share. The hard part is figuring out what they all are and how to share them in an impactful way. For some people it comes naturally. They just know their purpose.

Like my son for instance. From the age of four he's been saying he wants to be an engineer. Now that he is eleven, that hasn't changed. He has just added onto his vision by saying he wants to own his own engineering firm as well. He just knows.

Let me share with you some things that helped me on my path to becoming an unbreakable woman and learning to *#BeginWithBelief*.

I asked myself a question and I want you to do the same. What are four topics you can talk about for hours or write a book about? I want you to throw out all preconceived ideas of what you think you *should* be doing. Don't worry about what you got your degree in. If you don't want to work in that field, then so be it. You must allow space for your talent to flourish. Just think about any subjects that you can talk about for hours or that your friends often ask you about. My topics were:

- TRANSITIONING from bad girl to grown woman

- Being unbreakable through the storm
- Public Relations
- The hard part of parenting

So NOW I want to see what you've come up with. Take a picture and inbox me on Instagram! (@TinaSaidSo). Let's talk about it.

"The meaning of life is to find your gift. The purpose of life is to give your gift away."

ANOTHER THING that you can do to help you with your clarity is to think about repeat compliments that you have received. One thing that I have been complimented on for years is my writing. Writing in different formats has been easy for me since I was in the ninth grade. When I became a publicist six years ago it involved writing a lot of press releases. It would take me about three hours to get them right. Now it takes me about thirty minutes. Whenever they are put out to the public I get messages from other people about writing theirs. To tell a story about a stranger that is compelling, making people want to follow their journey and know more about them is a true gift that I take pride in possessing.

Another helpful clarity hack is meditation. Now this one is tricky if you are like me and you have a purposely annoying eleven-year-old and a four-year-old with an opinion. You have to use your time wisely. Finding that quiet time for yourself is so essential. It gives you that much needed time to reflect on how beautiful your unbreakable journey is. I am up at around four a.m. every morning. My body just turns on at that time. That's the time I use to meditate and recite my affirmations. It may be all just a mental trick, but it makes me feel so powerful and shows me a clear path to where I need to be. You should try it.

I want you to figure out what success means to you. The more specific you are about what you want the easier it is to receive it. Know what it is you're aiming for. Do you want to make $40,000 or $100,000 as an entrepreneur? Do you want a $10,000 raise at work by the end of the year? Whatever your revenue goal is, be specific. If it's not a monetary goal then how many clients do you want to have? However it is that you are measuring your success just make sure you are specific. What is success to you at this very moment?

One of the other things that is effective for a lot of people when building their future is creating a vision board. I always see flyers for vision board parties, especially at the turn of the year. So maybe you can find a group of like-minded women and learn how to effectively create your vision board.

No matter what it is you need to get clear on what

masterpiece you want to share with the world. I want you to be bold in your pursuit. So often, especially us women, we discount our inner greatness and our purpose because we don't feel that we are unique or special enough for the world to know about. Don't ever doubt your power because if the world didn't need you, you wouldn't be here. You were made to fill a void that can only be filled by you. Your purpose may not sound important to you but trust and believe, it has the potential to change someone's life. *You were destined for more.*

I want you to try something for me. Write a personal mission statement that puts your vision in writing. No matter what it is or how long it is, write it down. I will share mine with you.

MY MISSION IS **to remind women across the world that we are unbreakable and help them reach their highest level of greatness.**

HOW DOES it feel to see your mission in writing? Great, right? When you have found what you can comfortably share with the world, you no longer feel like you're losing. You know you haven't given up on yourself. That's the feeling you have when you have been working a job you hate for years. You can't shake the thought of that business that has been on your mind and in your heart for the past few years. It's like you are just disgusted until you decide to take that leap of faith, you have realized your purpose and etched out your vision. These are the only things that make you feel like you're living a fulfilled life. That is something I learned a long time ago from Dr. Myla Bennett. If you are doing something that is not aligned with your purpose it will never matter how much it is paying you; you will never be satisfied. Purpose is about how something makes you feel, so you can't put a dollar amount on it.

After you've created your vision and thought about your purpose, the next logical thing to do is to set your goals.

Action Step:

CREATE the vision in your mind then create a vision board. Make it a point to look at the vision board every single day. Select pictures for your vision board that correspond with what you have written down. Remember, the question you need to ask yourself is "What does success look and feel like to you?"

4

Set Goals and Crush Them

As you begin this journey to becoming an unbreakable woman, I want you to celebrate every single victory. Be happy for yourself any time you move forward because one new step is as powerful as a giant leap. If you're doing anything at all to work toward your dreams, that's progress. Identifying your goals, facing your fears, and deciding to *#BeginWithBelief* is a huge step in the right direction and will become the normal way of living for you.

"If you set your goals and go after them with all the

determination you can muster, your gifts will take you places that will amaze you."

The words of the great Les Brown.

HAVE you ever really thought about your goal? Maybe it was your goal to write a book. You have thought about it for the past year but for some reason it just hasn't happened? Why not? You think about it every day. It's a part of you.

Don't put your goals on the back burner. The best way to get to your goal is to figure out why you want it.

It's just like when you're in a dead-end relationship. Right in the middle of it you stop and ask yourself, *"Why the hell am I in this?"* If you don't identify why you want to complete a project or goal, then the same thing will happen. You will become deflated with defeat and just quit because there is no why. It must be something you deeply want, or you are positioning yourself for failure. Create a clear why so that you can be bold in your pursuit of your big goal.

Your why will help you demolish your excuses. Just like your home needs to be built on a good, solid foundation, so does your goal. Each one of us is different. We have different desires depending on our situation. You have to figure out what drives you. What is that true desire that sets your soul on fire? When we know exactly what we want and exactly why we want it, it makes us go the extra mile to push for the finish line.

"If it doesn't challenge you, it doesn't change you."

PEOPLE WHO HAVE BEEN in the same position for years tend to blame other people because they have not figured out how to advance in life. For you to take the steps to become who you want to be and leave the position you're in now, you have to get real with yourself. Some hard, ugly truths are going to have to be realized. The truth is, it's your own fault. Yes, I know that sounds harsh, but it's true. I had to realize this myself. Every choice you have ever made in your life has contributed to where you are in life now.

Be honest. Did you watch the entire season of *Orange Is the New Black* when it came out or do you make it a point to watch *Power* when it's on? At the same time do you complain that you don't have time to work on your dream or your business? I'm just asking you to get real. All of those hours could have been spent differently. We all have that one guilty pleasure. My guilty pleasure is Candy Crush. I literally used to wake up and play it. I have learned to control my addiction! Now, I only play one round per day. Hey, it's all about progress and honesty!

Although it can be quite challenging, you can't let your guilty pleasures completely distract you from accomplishing your goals.

"People with goals succeed because they know exactly where they're going."

I KNOW that sometimes you may set a colossal sized goal. I do that all the time as well, so I can relate. The trick that I have learned is to break that big goal into mini goals. So, 1 goal really becomes eight different goals. That way even the overall goal becomes more attainable. You will get to reward yourself and be happy for yourself every time you accomplish one of your smaller goals. That's the only way I was able to write this book. I had to break it down just like this:

DAY 1: Decide on title
    Day 2: Decide on chapter topics
    Day 3: Make openings for each chapter
    Day 4: Expound on chapter 1
    Day 5: Expound on chapter 2
    Day 6: Finish chapter 1
    Day 7: Expound on chapter 3

Day 8-Expound on chapter 4

Day 9-Finish Chapter 2

I DID this all the way until the final chapter. You can even mark your dates on a calendar. Had I not broken it down, I would have probably given up due to frustration. You have to set your goals according to how you're most comfortable because the last thing I want you to do is quit. Creating your blueprint turns your simple thought into an actual vision. You will get rid of any uncertainty about your project.

Set hard deadlines for yourself by putting actual dates beside your mini goals. Deadlines create a sense of urgency that will always eliminate procrastination. One of the best apps to use to keep your thoughts in order, create a checklist, and set deadlines is Evernote. It has been a life saver for me since I was introduced to it over a year ago.

One thing that may help you in reaching your goal is an accountability partner. Some people like to have a life coach as well. It just depends on whatever is best for you. Tell a trusted friend or family member what you're trying to accomplish and give them updates. Here is where I put my son to work. Kids are so honest. When I take him to school in the morning I will talk to him about what I need to have done by his bedtime that night. He never forgets to ask me if I've done it. This gives me the drive to keep pushing forward even when I don't feel like it. One, because I don't want to feel like I'm disappointing him. Two, I don't want him to have to ask me why I haven't done the task. Lastly, because his honesty is ridiculous. If he calls me lazy or something for not completing the task I'm going into full mom mode with one of the "Do you know how many hours of labor I was in with you" speeches.

Whoever it is you have as an accountability partner make sure they help you celebrate your wins too! You have to make sure you have the right kind of energy around you.

"The best view comes after the hardest climb."

MOTIVATION IS the energy that drives you. With the right motivation you can accomplish anything. It is integral to your success. Many things can affect your motivation. When you hit any bump in the road that may seem to bring you down, keep your eye on the end result. Keep your positive energy intact. If ever you feel overwhelmed put your goals in order of importance and do one thing at a time. That will help get you back on track and not get distracted.

I have noticed that sometimes when I look at all the missed calls I have and start to call people back they always tell me that they have been trying so hard to reach me. When I ask them what they wanted it's always that they just wanted to see what I was doing because they're at home bored. WHAT? That is the whole reason I decided to start turning my ringer off when I'm working on anything related to me accomplishing my goals. I schedule my time appropriately. I block myself from my phone. You probably think I'm joking, but no. I use the *Flipd* app to block myself from getting on social media or anything else on my phone. Sometimes you just have to put a do not disturb button on your life in order to get things done.

So, the final thing I want to discuss with you about your goals and your blueprint is to keep an open mind. If you're doing everything you feel that you're supposed to be doing but still can't seem to generate results, what do you think may be the issue? Are you so comfortable with your plan that you refuse to tweak it? Don't let your pride stand in the way of new, great ideas. Don't allow yourself to keep struggling with no results. Having tunnel vision will make you miss opportunities. I want you to reevaluate your plans every three weeks just to make sure that they still make sense.

Bonus:

Powerful Goal Setting Formula

As YOU READ and begin to practice this strategy, I want you to see and feel yourself in possession right now of the end result. I got this from one of my coaches, Michael Baptiste. This will work for you if you apply this persistently and consistently. I recommend three times per day; morning when you first rise, just after lunch or during the afternoon, and at night just before bed. Don't reveal your thoughts to anyone. Solely focus only on the end result and within sixty days you will begin to see the change occurring in your life.

On This Day, September 2, 2019, the time is now 1:22 am. I'm sitting in my comfy purple velvet office chair at my nice wooden desk. As I logged into my bank account I can see that I've made over $10,000 (Insert your desired number here) since I last checked.

I can feel the cool AC blowing on my skin, but my heater is on my feet! I can feel my white silk robe on my arms and legs. I can see my pretty white carpet underneath me. I feel my cool laptop underneath my hands as they both relax over the keyboard. I take a deep breath, and as I do, I feel a powerful electricity like energy flow through my body, causing goosebumps and making me super excited. As time now seems to stand still for one moment, I realize that I have just stepped into my dream, and made it become a reality.

My life is more amazing than I ever imagined. I stand up from my chair with my soft white carpet underneath by bare feet and I raise my hands in praise. I'm feeling absolutely amazing and incredibly grateful now that I've reached my goal and surpassed it. I can't believe how easy it was to earn over $10,000 in profits

last month. It's as if I'm a money magnet, and money is just flowing to me daily in avalanches of abundance – effortlessly.

To reward myself for earning $10,000 in profits for the month of August, I am going to plan a trip to another country for myself, my husband, and my four children. In addition, for

me and only me, I am going to buy myself a new car. I am going to pay my aunt's and my in-law's mortgage for this month. I will continue to give glory to God and keep my faith on full. I love my life.

Action Step:

Now it's your turn.

REMEMBER YOUR WHY.

What are the 3 biggest reasons why you MUST reach your goal?

1.

2.

3.

. . .

GIVE yourself a few hours to really answer this question.

THE PURPOSE of this exercise is to gain absolute clarity on why you're doing what you're doing. When times get hard your WHY is going to push you past temporary setbacks and defeats.

5

Get up and get it!

So many times, people decide against starting something because the fear of failure creeps in. That fear is so powerful that it outshines the passion. That's a big problem. I don't want you to think that it's not normal to feel fear. You just have to learn to admit that your fear is holding you back from your accomplishments. So how exactly does your fear decide to show up? That's important for you to know so that you can easily recognize it and attack it. Some of the fear factors that I've experienced in the past are procrastination and being overwhelmed.

Usually when you begin to procrastinate and put less important things in front of the ultimate goal, it's a sign that you are fearful of the outcome. The same is true for feeling overwhelmed. When you make yourself believe that there is way too much on your plate, so you talk yourself into not doing anything at all because everything is stressful. Fear is forever going to be there, it's your job to control it. You just have to break that hold it has on you and stop letting it rob you of your success.

For me, I didn't want to be a person that was filled with regret because I didn't just go for it; Whatever *it* was. People start to make excuses as to why their new and better life can't happen. Many times, we blame it on a lack of money, lack of skills, or lack of adequate resources as the reasons why we're stuck in our same situations. Every one of us has the basic resources we need to improve our quality of life. Once you start focusing on what you lack, that's when you forfeit the fight. You've already programmed yourself to think you've lost.

"There is no illusion greater than fear."

YOU HAVE to go after whatever it is you want with an attitude of a winner. You have to fight defeat because no one else will do it for you. If you're sitting back and waiting for an opportunity to be placed in front of you then you're making a big mistake. Life will pass you by and you will never have truly lived up to your full potential because you were afraid to create your opportunity, go for it, and *#BeginWithBelief*. You have to fall in love with your idea of a better life and motivate yourself to keep going. Motivation is the magic behind greatness.

I want you to know what it is that makes you get up and go. Don't spend time worrying about anyone else and what they may say. It's a sad place to be in to worry so much about what other people will think of you, to worry if people will buy your product, or any other excuse that fear has allowed you to conjure up. We listen to the noise around us. It is important for you to temporarily tune the world out. You can't pay attention to everyone else's thoughts or even consider their opinions. Don't let all the noise around you deter you from your path. What do I mean by noise?

Simply think about when the water is running at home. Maybe someone is washing dishes. You can easily hear it running and it's a little annoying, but eventually it's like you become accustomed to the sound. You're hearing that same sound for so long you just get used to it.

Everyone has that noise that needs to be ignored. That noise of the same people telling them repeatedly what it is they can't do. Your capabilities are not based on whatever you have not accomplished over the past few years. Your capabilities are based on the heart you have right now to move forward and get things done. So, ignore those who say you can't. That noise is only another element that blocks you from reaching your goals. It's imperative that you stay on your path and remain ambitious. Don't worry about the scary part of your journey that everyone has pointed out to you. Just do it. Failing is not going to take you out of the game. Not being in the game at all means you've already lost.

When my husband, Tracey, and I moved to Atlanta all we had was faith. Tracey had lived in Virginia his entire life and I lived there for the majority of mine. It would be a lie for me to say I wasn't questioning the decision as I started driving my car behind the U-Haul. What if this feeling of love is temporary? What if we don't enjoy each other's company as much as we think we do? What if I can't tolerate the strange sounds he makes when he sleeps? (This one is still in question).

At that time my mom still had her house in Virginia, so I was thinking about how it wasn't too late to turn back. I couldn't do that though. I already knew what life was like in Richmond. I needed a change. I needed better and I was determined to get it. I had to realize that fear was nothing more than dumb scenarios that I created in my own mind.

We've all experienced it. We often put ourselves in the state of panic for no reason. Don't add extra stress to yourself by worrying about things that are completely out of your control. You have the power to choose exactly what you believe and think. I had to execute my faith.

Luckily, we both took the risk. People who don't take risks will never advance. Just take the shot and don't take your failures personally. You better find the kid in you! You know how kids do the exact opposite of what they're told because of that unshakable curiosity? When we tell them not to touch the stove, but they still want to touch it because they want to find out just how hot it is. When they are told not to go into the deep end of the water at the pool, but it looks like the other kids are living their best lives over there, so they sneak over there anyway. They can stare straight in the face of fear. Be that kid again. The only way to challenge it is to actively participate in it.

Whenever there is a time when you think about giving it all up just keep in mind that any unfired shot is a missed shot. It's ok to *shoot your shot* and miss because at least you tried. What keeps successful people in the game is that they take their failures and improve upon them. Your failures are the best invitation for you to start over again from the beginning with all the new knowledge you have. It stops you from being lazy and doing only what you need to do to get by.

It's like having your alarm go off in the morning. A fresh

new day, a fresh new chance. Think about this. When Sidney
Poitier first auditioned for the American Negro Theater, he
messed up his lines and spoke in a heavy Caribbean accent,
which made the director angrily tell him to stop wasting his
time and go get a job as a dishwasher.

Poitier worked on his craft and eventually became a
hugely successful Hollywood star. He won an Academy
Award for Best Actor (Lilies of the Field, 1963) and helped
break down the color barrier in the American film industry.

A young Jay-Z couldn't get any record label to sign him.
Growing up in the Marcy Projects in Brooklyn, Jay-Z worked
to perfect his flow, his lyrics, and his references. When he
couldn't get a single bite on his first CD, he and his friends
sold the CD out of their car. The rapper — who's also an
investor and entrepreneur — is worth more than $1 billion,
according to Forbes.

How about this one: a young Henry Ford ruined his repu-
tation with a couple of failed automobile businesses.
However, after conducting a search, he was finally able to
find a partner who had faith in him. Ford proved he had
learned from his mistakes when Ford Motor Company
forever changed the automotive industry and culture with
his assembly line mode of production. I gave you three exam-
ples to show you that failing forward means learning from
your mistakes and evolving from them.

After each failure just think of yourself as being reborn!

When we are babies and we haven't been exposed to the world's failure or success, unlike adults who spend a lot of time planning to avoid failure, babies simply experiment with new tasks. This leads to constant improvement. Every single day we are presented with great opportunities that come disguised as big, undefinable obstacles. You have to transform them to work in your favor rather than your failure.

"Feel the fear and do it anyway."

RIGHT NOW, I want you to make a list of all the lies you have told yourself. Any excuse that you have made that stops you from moving forward and loving life. After you have done that I want you to contradict the hell out of each one of those fearful thoughts.

For example: If you said, *"I don't have the* it *factor*, I want you to say; *"I am enough."* Or if your statement was, *"I am ashamed of my weight,"* then your contradicting statement would be, *"I am becoming more and more healthy every day."*

The reason I'm forcing you to do this is because you have probably fooled yourself into believing that you don't deserve those things you really want. If you feel like that then you will never have them. I am making you create a positive change in your mind. So right now, I want you to make a commitment to yourself every single day. I need you to wake up and go to sleep everyday saying one of your contradictory phrases. I would suggest standing right in front of the mirror and saying it with a smile!

WE'RE NOT DONE. I want you to look at the goals you have written down. I want you to write down two positive outcomes for each of them. I want you to shift your perspective on any fear of failing by removing the possibility of failure which may be at the forefront, blocking you from taking inspired action. You are creating a win-win situation for yourself. You are going to look at these positive outcomes every night before you go to bed and every morning when you wake up. You may think it seems dumb now, but it's going to change you and give you so much joy. You won't even remember any of the negative things that you were thinking before.

Action Step:

THINK about the noise you have around you. Write down the names of those who have deterred you from following your passion. Make it your point to avoid these people. If it's impossible to ignore them completely then avoid the conversation you have about your goals with them. It's up to you to get started on bettering your life. Don't forget to write your positive outcomes as well as your contradictory phrases! I'm so proud of you.

6

How can anyone see how great you are if you can't see it yourself?

Make sure you love yourself. That sounds easy but there are many people who continue to talk down on themselves every day without even realizing it. You must watch your words carefully because negative words become self-fulfilling prophecies. Our thoughts are so powerful that they control how we function which will determine how likely we are to achieve our goals.

You don't have to wait for anyone to tell you that you're beautiful, smart, funny, successful or anything else. Tell yourself.

I know we have all experienced some type of rejection that has made us believe that other people's words are true, but they are not. I understand. Most of us have been broken up when people that we wanted to be our friends don't accept us. Even when you're in college and you want to join an organization but you're not accepted into it, you feel stuck wondering why. You begin to think you're not good enough. Sometimes people even begin to compare themselves to others. I said sometimes, but that happens very often. There comes a time when you have to look at those other people and realize that they are no different from you. They had an idea just like you. The difference between you and them is that they acted. They weren't necessarily more talented or smarter than you, they were just more determined. They blatantly said *"F you"* to their excuses and refused to stop walking in their destiny.

Give yourself a break. When you begin to compare yourself to others, it becomes easy for your confidence to be broken. Other people will know when you're not confident. Aside from your physical attributes, your confidence is what attracts other people to you. People can recognize a confident woman the moment she walks into the room. If you come in speaking softly, not making eye contact, and look afraid to start conversations with other people, then your showing me and everyone else that you lack confidence. Becoming confident involves breaking out of the self-imposed prison that you call your comfort zone. Trust me, your greatness won't be activated there.

"Once you start believing in yourself, magic will start happening."

NONE of us are born with confidence, it's a skill we develop the same as learning to walk. Our childhood experiences all shape how much we believe in ourselves. Your level of confidence can change throughout the duration of your life. It's all based on the different things that happen to us that change the way we view the world, rather it be friendships, relationships, or general life events.

Regardless of your past, self-perception or personality, if you want to be confident you can be. Even if your childhood wasn't perfect, even if you were made fun of as a child, you can always take the steps necessary to improve the love you have for yourself. When you are confident you will believe that you can achieve anything. Even when you fail it won't seem so bad. It is our duty to develop a solid foundation of self-confidence that will stay intact despite any disappointments, hardships, or struggles.

Before you can begin to believe in your ability to carry

out any goal you have set, you have to know yourself better than anyone else.

Know what makes you unique and what you do well. When you are using your strengths to your advantage then your confidence level increases. On the flip side of that, if you know your weaknesses then you know what you need to work on to make yourself successful and ultimately make you more confident in that area.

One of the most helpful things to boost your confidence is preparation. Once you have prepared for something for so long you become extremely confident in your ability to deliver. This is like when your parents always tell you that practice makes perfect.

When I was younger (ages seven to eighteen) I was a swimmer. I practiced every single day except Sunday, even in the winter time. Whenever it was time for me to compete I was so cool and confident because I knew I practiced hard. My confidence allowed me to believe in myself and win. Me being a swimmer is what introduced me to true self confidence.

The very first time I went swimming I almost drowned. I went into the five foot depth at age six with my cousin. She tried to let me go, not remembering that I had never been in a pool before. I immediately wrapped my arms around her neck to keep myself up thinking she was fine. Long story short, the lifeguard had to save both of us. I didn't let that one incident stop me from being great. I practiced swimming that whole summer. The following summer is when I excelled and didn't stop until my teenage years. I went on to set records and ultimately dominate in the sport. Practice and confidence. I refused to let what happened before keep me away from my greatness.

"Confidence Breeds Strength"

THERE ARE many people who feel defeated before they even start because they have failed before and are afraid to fail again. Those negative memories of how you messed up can be affecting your confidence. Your bad experience absolutely cannot be the reason you won't move forward. It's a new day! The only time I want you to look so far back in your past is to celebrate the fact that you have made it so far ahead. Learn to appreciate all the struggles you've had because they have molded you into the unbreakable being you are today.

To become an unbreakable woman you have to remove *"I can't"* from your vocabulary. Instead of saying, "I can't," I need you to say, *"Why the hell can't I?"* Be determined to succeed in whatever goal you have set for yourself.

Just so you know, I'm not saying that every single minute of every single day you can show no fear. Don't live under the illusion that you will go into every situation with a mountain of confidence. Even the most confident people have moments where they are put into less than comfortable situations. You won't be an exception. Approach everything with a positive attitude. Being pessimistic will prevent you from feeling good about yourself when you actually accomplish something good.

Action Step:

STOP MINIMIZING YOUR PERSONAL VALUE. Understand that confidence and self-esteem let us know exactly how we feel about ourselves and can affect our lives. Write down all the things you have already accomplished so that you can remind yourself of how great you really are.

"Progress is impossible without change."

T he first step to fixing something is the actual realization that something is wrong. I have seen the strongest women break down and suffer from extreme sadness. In some cases, it was them coming from an extreme high point in their life where they were very popular, money was flowing, and life was simply good. When a change came they really weren't equipped to handle it. They began to blame others for their downfall.

"Change Begins with You"

FOR ANYTHING to ever change for you, you have to accept who you are or what you have done and make the change within yourself. How will you see success if you don't take the time to work on you? You want to see quick results within your business life or your work life, but you're not even taking the time to actually be a good person with a clean heart. I told you before, everything that has ever happened to you is a result of the things you have done. That is nothing to be ashamed of.

Have you ever thought about the act of forgiveness? I used to think it was crap when people would say to forgive someone because ultimately it helps you to move on. I was like no, I'm still mad! As I grew up I fully understood. You can't base your circumstances or your feelings on what someone else has done to you. I read a book called The Four Agreements. I highly recommend it to you. It changed my entire perspective on life as a whole. That's just how powerful it is.

As it relates to forgiveness, it taught me not to take anything personally. It's so funny because for years my husband had a yellow piece of notebook paper taped to our bathroom mirror. He had handwritten the words "Don't Take Anything Personally." I only really looked at it when we disagreed on something. I had to remind myself that it was okay that he didn't understand at that moment why I was always right! I didn't pay attention to the signs daily until after I read The Four Agreements. It said not to take anything personally because nothing others do is because of you.

What others say and do is a projection of their own life. We take things personally when we agree with what others have said. When we do not agree, the things that others say cannot affect us emotionally. When we do not care about what others think about us, their words or behavior cannot affect us. When someone yells at you, gossips about you, harms you, it still is not about you! Their actions and words are based on what they believe in their personal life.

Our personal belief system makes us feel safe. When people have beliefs that are different from our own, we get scared, defend ourselves, and try to impose our point of view on them. When someone gets angry with us it is because our belief system is challenging their belief system and they get scared. They need to defend their point of view. Do not become angry, create conflict, and expend energy arguing when you are aware of this.

Practice forgiveness. It is a promise not a feeling. Forgiveness is a promise not to use the past sin against them or yourself. We can determine our future by what we focus on. Learning to truly forgive yourself and others will empower you. The way you know you have forgiven someone is if you can wish them well or say you are grateful for them and mean it. Don't block your own blessings holding onto negativity.

Empowering yourself is so important. You can't ALWAYS look to others to be your motivation or inspiration. Even when thinking about your why you must be motivated in knowing that your why can't wait. Self-motivation is the best there is. When you are only empowered or inspired by other people that means you are solely dependent on others. I want you to remain excited about your life long after those people are out of your presence.

Have you ever heard the saying that your bank account is as big as your library? Knowing that your mind determines who you are, you should want to feed your mind every single day. I was scrolling through Facebook the other day and I saw that someone posed a question that said, *"Can you be a great publicist if you suffer from social anxiety?"*

Well, for those that know me well, they know I'm a homebody. I spend my time at home on my sofa or in front of my computer with my heater on my feet. I don't like going to movie theaters, we have Netflix and Hulu. I don't like going out to dinner, my husband is an amazing cook. I don't like going to parties because people are crazy. I have kids to come home to. See? Homebody. It's where I'm most comfortable. That's crazy that I ended up in the entertainment industry and a publicist, nonetheless. We get invited to everything. Most of the events are celebrity filled with cameras everywhere. We also host a bunch of events. When I say "we" I'm talking about myself and my team/family at *The epiMediaGroup*, Quincy Griggs who is the Project Liaison and Ebony Porter-Ike who is the President and Founder and one of my inspirations.

So, me being a loner, it was completely out of my world when I began my career as a Publicist. I mean that was the whole reason I didn't want to be in radio. I hate the attention. But that hasn't affected my ability to help build amazing brands, handle celebrity publicity, and help produce amazing events.

So, the answer was yes. You can do *anything* despite *anything*. I always feed my brain. I'm a huge fan of books so I knew that. I was always reading both fiction and nonfiction books that took me to a place where I can relate to characters who were like me and stepped out of the box. Even self-help books that gave advice for introverts like me. Books helped propel me to new levels. There's no way in a million years that I ever thought I had the IT factor to work with the Braxton family or create bodies of work that even had Russell Simmons or Floyd Mayweather's names attached to it. It was beyond my wildest dreams. So when I hear that saying about your bank account being as big as your library I don't take that lightly. Feed your mind and help yourself develop into an unbreakable being.

Personal development isn't just a one-time thing. You must commit to yourself and make yourself better every day, even if it's only for an hour per day. Whether it's reading a book, listening to a self-help tape, or watching a movie like *The Secret*, use whatever you need to help you to constantly strengthen your mind, do it.

Now, what action are you taking to become The Unbreakable Woman that you were created to be?